These notes refer to the House of Lords (Cessation of Membership) Bill [HL] as introduced in the House of Lords on 17th May 2012 [HL Bill 21]

HOUSE OF LORDS
(CESSATION OF MEMBERSHIP) BILL [HL]

EXPLANATORY NOTES

INTRODUCTION

1. These Explanatory Notes relate to the House of Lords (Cessation of Membership) Bill [HL] as introduced in the House of Lords on 17th May 2012. They have been prepared by Lord Steel of Aikwood in order to assist the reader of the Bill and to help inform debate on it. They do not form part of the Bill and have not been endorsed by Parliament.

2. The Notes should be read in conjunction with the Bill. They are not, and are not meant to be, a comprehensive description of the Bill. So where a clause or part of a clause does not seem to require any explanation or comment, none is given.

BACKGROUND AND SUMMARY

3. At present, a person who is made a "life peer" under the Life Peerages Act 1958 remains a member of the House of Lords for life; and the same is true of those hereditary peers who remain or become members of the House of Lords under the House of Lords Act 1999.

4. The Bill provides for membership of the House of Lords to come to an end in three classes of case: (a) peers who choose to retire; (b) peers who fail to attend or obtain leave of absence for the whole of a Parliamentary Session; and (c) peers who are convicted of serious criminal offences.

These notes refer to the House of Lords (Cessation of Membership) Bill [HL] as introduced in the House of Lords on 17th May 2012 [HL Bill 21]

COMMENTARY ON CLAUSES

Clause 1—Retirement

5. Clause 1 allows peers to retire from membership of the House of Lords. Retirement is a permanent decision that cannot later be rescinded.

6. The precise legal consequences of ceasing to be a member of the House are specified in clause 4.

7. The word "peer" is used in this clause and elsewhere in the Bill so as to include both persons on whom a life peerage has been conferred under the Life Peerages Act 1958 and also those hereditary peers who remain or become members of the House of Lords by virtue of section 2 of the House of Lords Act 1999. Bishops are not peers: they are Lords of Parliament who attend the House of Lords by virtue of their office; provision is made elsewhere about retirement and discipline of Bishops.

Clause 2—Non-attendance

8. Clause 2 provides that a peer who does not attend the House during the whole of a Parliamentary Session ceases to be a member of the House, unless he or she has obtained the House's "leave of absence" under its Standing Orders.

9. Attendance at any Committee proceedings counts as attendance for these purposes; but not mere presence in the Palace of Westminster.

10. The legal consequences of ceasing to be a member of the House are specified in clause 4.

Clause 3—Conviction of serious offence

11. Clause 3 provides for peers to be excluded from the House if convicted of a criminal offence which is sufficiently serious to attract a sentence of one year's imprisonment or more. The clause applies to conviction for offences whether in the United Kingdom or elsewhere (although the House has the power to resolve to disapply the clause to a non-United Kingdom conviction in special circumstances).

12. If a conviction or sentence is overturned on appeal, the exclusion from the House is cancelled (subsection (4)).

13. The legal consequences of ceasing to be a member of the House are specified in clause 4.

*These notes refer to the House of Lords (Cessation of Membership) Bill [HL]
as introduced in the House of Lords on 17th May 2012 [HL Bill 21]*

Clause 4—Effect of ceasing to be a member

14. Clause 4 sets out the legal effects of the earlier provisions of the Bill that provide for persons to cease to be members of the House in specified circumstances.

15. In essence, a peer who retires or is excluded under the Bill cannot attend the House of Lords, but becomes eligible to vote in elections for, and to be elected to, the House of Commons.

16. A person to whom the Bill applies remains a peer, and the Bill does not affect a person's title, or any other incident of peerage apart from membership of the House of Lords. Matters such as access to premises and facilities will continue to be determined by the House.

17. The House of Lords already has power to suspend members, and the Bill does not interfere with that.

Clause 5—Certificate of Lord Speaker

18. The provisions of the Bill about non-attendance and conviction of offences are activated by certificate of the Lord Speaker. Clause 5 makes it clear that decisions about certificates cannot be challenged in the courts (being matters of Parliamentary privilege) and that the Lord Speaker can take action whether or not anyone has made a request.

Clauses 6 to 8

19. Clauses 6 to 8 are technical. They provide for the Bill to come into force immediately and to apply to the whole of the United Kingdom.

HOUSE OF LORDS (CESSATION OF MEMBERSHIP) BILL [HL]

EXPLANATORY NOTES

These notes refer to the House of Lords (Cessation of Membership) Bill [HL] as introduced in the House of Lords on 17th May 2012
[HL Bill 21]

Order to be Printed,
25th June 2012

© Parliamentary copyright House of Lords 2012

This publication may be reproduced under the terms of the Parliamentary Click-Use Licence, available online through the National Archives website at
www.nationalarchives.gov.uk/information-management/our-services/parliamentary-licence-information.htm
Enquiries to The National Archives, Kew, Richmond, Surrey, TW9 4DU; email: psi@nationalarchives.gsi.gov.uk

PUBLISHED BY AUTHORITY OF THE HOUSE OF LORDS

LONDON – THE STATIONERY OFFICE LIMITED

Printed in the United Kingdom by
The Stationery Office Limited

£1.50

HL Bill 21—EN   (21416)   55/2

PEFC
PEFC/16-33-622

ISBN 978-0-10-847508-5
9 780108 475085